E S T A T E   P U

SCUNTHORPE

BROUGHTON

C000196245

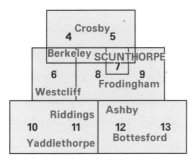

ROAD MAP   pages 2-3
ENLARGED CENTRE   page 7
INDEX TO STREETS   pages 14-16

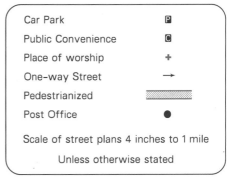

Every effort has been made to verify
the accuracy of information in this book
but the publishers cannot accept
responsibility for expense or loss caused
by any error or omission. Information
that will be of assistance to the user
of the maps will be welcomed.

The representation of a road, track or
footpath on the maps in this atlas is no
evidence of the existence of a right
of way.

Car Park	P
Public Convenience	C
Place of worship	+
One-way Street	→
Pedestrianized	/////
Post Office	●

Scale of street plans 4 inches to 1 mile

Unless otherwise stated

Street plans prepared and published by ESTATE PUBLICATIONS, Bridewell House,
Tenterden, Kent, and based upon the ORDNANCE SURVEY maps with the
sanction of the controller of H.M. Stationery Office

The publishers acknowledge the co-operation of the local
authorities of towns represented in this atlas.

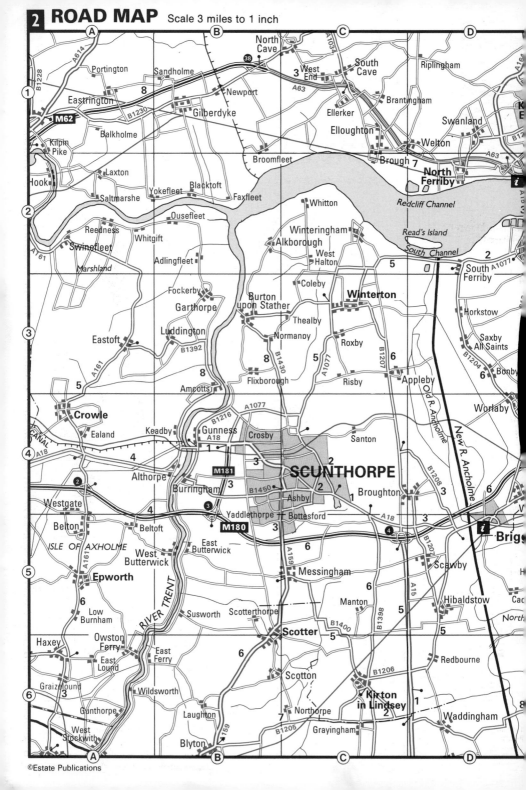

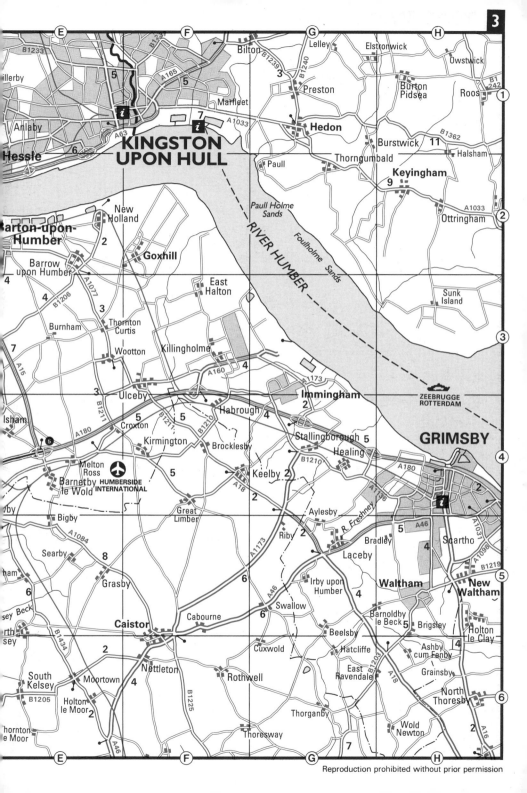

LYSAGHTS WY
BILLET LA
B1430
LYSAGHTS ENTERPRISE PARK
Conesby Farm
A1077
FOXHILLS INDUSTRIAL ESTATE
POLA WY
MERCIA WY
Warehouse
ORB LANE
Works
St Vincents AV
Crosby Warren
St Vincent House
WYBECK RD
Works
CLAYFIELD RD
PHOENIX PARKWAY   MANNABERG   WAY
WINTERTON WAY
PIPPINGDALE RD
CROSBY ROAD
BUCKINGHAM AVENUE
FLIXBOROUGH FOOTPATH
SAWCLIFFE INDUSTRIAL PARK
NEWCOMEN WAY
HARGREAVES
WINTERTON ROAD
SHEFFIELD PARK AV
Playing Field
CHATTERS CR
ABBEY GDS
AJAX
BESSEMER WAY
FERRY ROAD
ROAD WEST
OLD CROSBY
WARREN
Works
GROSVENOR ST
NORMANBY ROAD
ROAD
Works
Ambulance Station
Timber Yard
Warehouse
Works
HORNSBY CRES
BUCKINGHAM AV NTH
SPENCE ST
DETUYLL ST
DIANA ST
BURKE ST
DIGBY ST
MULGRAVE ST
SHEFFIELD ST
WINTERTON ROAD
BRIGG ROAD
GDS
THEDBORNE
LONG RD
DIGBY ST
DALE ST
SHEFF RD WEST ST
Schs
BUCKINGHAM ST STH
SHEFFIELD ST
STREET
SHEFFIELD STREET
NORTH ST
GEORGE ST
CROSBY ROAD
GLEBE   ROAD
KING ST
KINGS ST
NORTH ST
HOME ST
CROSS ST
TRAFFORD ST
DAWES   LANE
School
Playing Field
KIMBERLEY ST
ALBERT ST
PERCIVAL ST
TEALE ST
NELL ST
GILLIATT ST
WELLS ST
Sch
Cemy
KING ST
Mkt
CHURCH
Library
C
CARLTON ST
HIGH STREET
Supermarket
SMITH STREET
PORTER ST
FOX ST
WEST ST
Crosby
PARKINSON AV
CLARKE ST
ALLANBY ST
FRANCES ST
CHAPEL ST
ROBERT ST
BELGRAVE
JOHN ST
Bus Sta
FENTON ST
Leisure Centre
Bowls Centre
STATION RD
IRONSIDE ROAD
CASTELLA
ALEXANDER APPROACH
DONCASTER
HENRY ST
GERVASE ST
DEYNE AV
OSWALD RD
DUNSTALL ST
LANEHAM ST
ARGYLE ST
LINDUM ST
THOMPSON ST
Rec Grd
STATION ROAD
A1029
BLUEBELL CL
ROSE WLK
LAVENDER
HARMAN
LEONARD CRES
EXETER ST
BRUCE ST
MAR RD
CLIFF GARDENS
CORPORATION STREET
RAVENDALE ST
Police H.Q.
Fire Sta
RAVENDALE ST

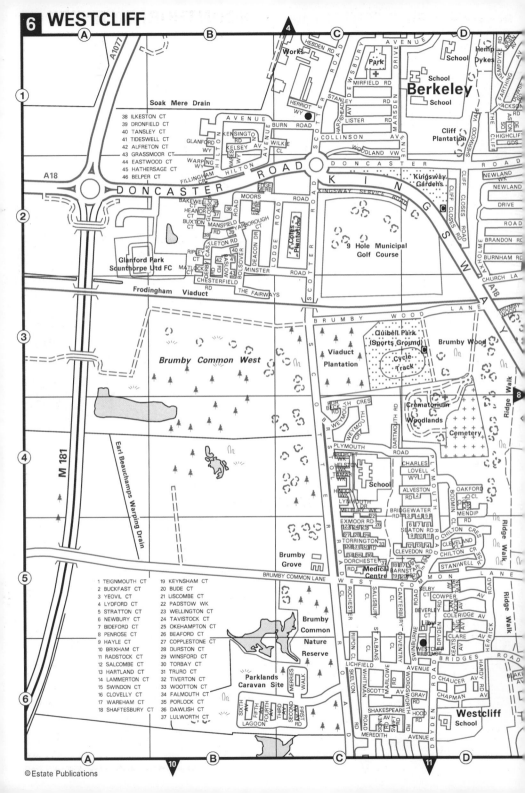

6 WESTCLIFF

Soak Mere Drain

38 ILKESTON CT
39 DRONFIELD CT
40 TANSLEY CT
41 TIDESWELL CT
42 ALFRETON CT
43 GRASSMOOR CT
44 EASTWOOD CT
45 HATHERSAGE CT
46 BELPER CT

Works

Park

School

Berkeley

School

School

Hemp Dykes

Cliff Plantation

A1077

A18

DONCASTER ROAD

KINGSWAY

KINGSWAY SERVICE ROAD

Kingsway Gardens

Newland Wk
Newland Drive
Road
Brandon Rd
Burnham Rd
Church La

A18

Collinson Avenue

Woodland Vw

9 Hole Municipal Golf Course

Coves Plantation

Frodingham Viaduct

THE FAIRWAYS

M 181

Earl Beauchamps Warping Drain

Brumby Common West

Viaduct Plantation

Quibell Park (Sports Ground)

Cycle Track

Brumby Wood

Crematorium Woodlands

Cemetery

Ridge Walk

School

Brumby Grove

BRUMBY COMMON LANE

1 TEIGNMOUTH CT
2 BUCKFAST CT
3 YEOVIL CT
4 LYDFORD CT
5 STRATTON CT
6 NEWBURY CT
7 BIDEFORD CT
8 PENROSE CT
9 HAYLE CT
10 BRIXHAM CT
11 RADSTOCK CT
12 SALCOMBE CT
13 HARTLAND CT
14 LAMMERTON CT
15 SWINDON CT
16 CLOVELLY CT
17 WAREHAM CT
18 SHAFTESBURY CT

19 KEYNSHAM CT
20 BUDE CT
21 LISCOMBE CT
22 PADSTOW WK
23 WELLINGTON CT
24 TAVISTOCK CT
25 OKEHAMPTON CT
26 BEAFORD CT
27 COPPLESTONE CT
28 DURSTON CT
29 WINSFORD CT
30 TORBAY CT
31 TRURO CT
32 TIVERTON CT
33 WOOTTON CT
34 FALMOUTH CT
35 PORLOCK CT
36 DAWLISH CT
37 LULWORTH CT

Brumby Common Nature Reserve

Parklands Caravan Site

Medical Centre

Liby

WESTCLIFF PRECINCT

Westcliff School

Ridge Walk

© Estate Publications

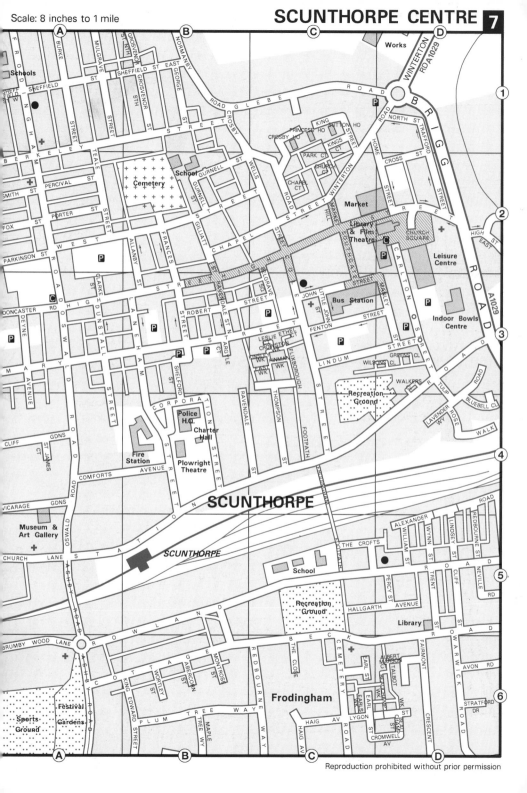

SCUNTHORPE

SCUNTHORPE

Frodingham

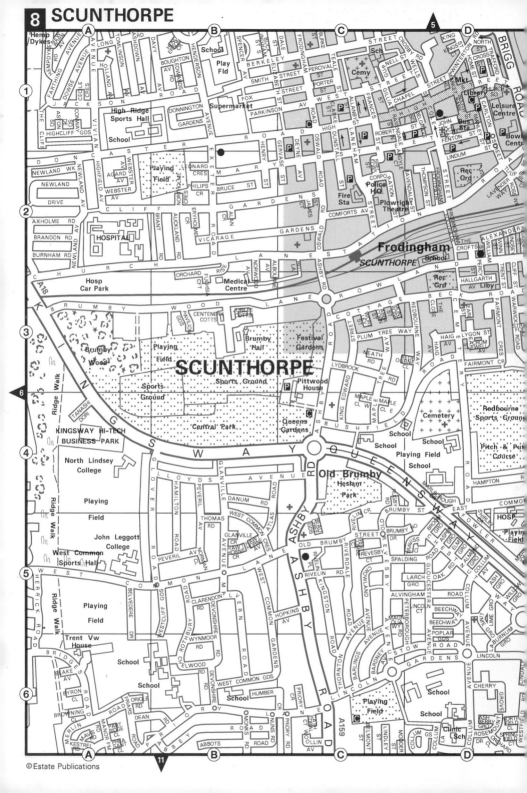

8 SCUNTHORPE

© Estate Publications

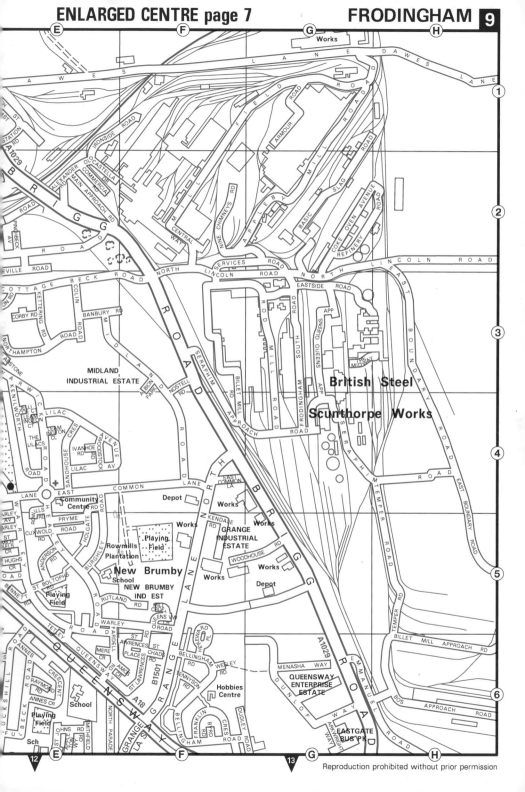

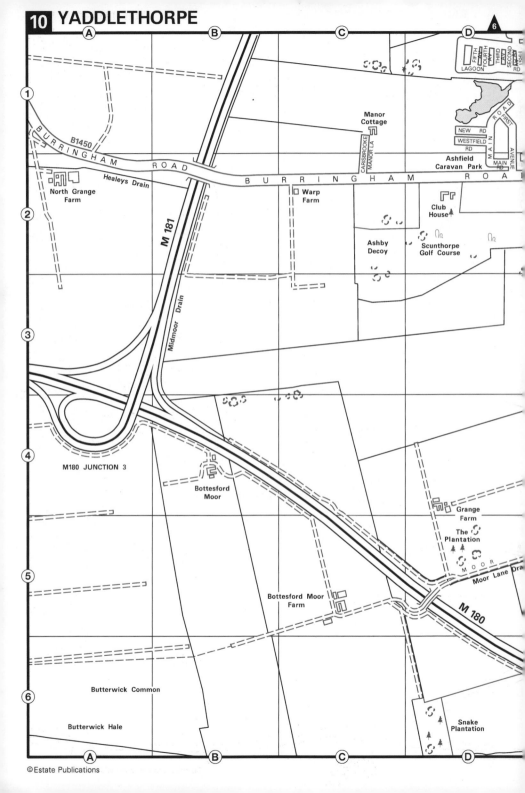

A B C D

6

1

FIFTH FOURTH THIRD SECOND FIRST RD
LAGOON

BURRINGHAM B1450 ROAD

Manor Cottage

NEW RD
WESTFIELD RD

MAIN ROAD

FIRST AVENUE

Ashfield Caravan Park

Healeys Drain

BURRINGHAM ROAD

MAIN RD

North Grange Farm

2

M 181

Warp Farm

Club House

Ashby Decoy

Scunthorpe Golf Course

Midmoor Drain

3

4

M180 JUNCTION 3

Bottesford Moor

Grange Farm

The Plantation

MOOR

Moor Lane Drain

5

Bottesford Moor Farm

M 180

6

Butterwick Common

Snake Plantation

Butterwick Hale

A B C D

© Estate Publications

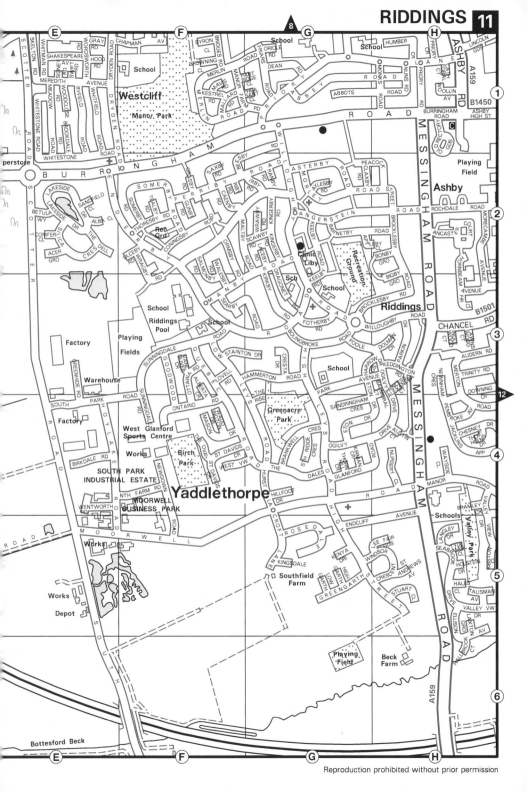

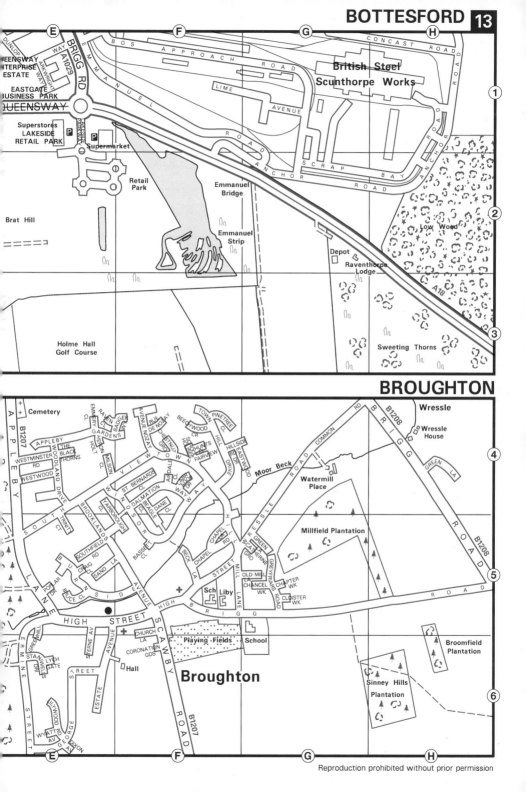

BOTTESFORD
13

British Steel
Scunthorpe Works

CONCAST ROAD

BOS APPROACH ROAD

LIME AVENUE

EMMANUEL ROAD

ANCHOR ROAD

SCRAP BAY

A18

E
BRIGG RD A1029
DUNLOP
EASTWRIGHT
PARKWRIGHT
WAY

QUEENSWAY ENTERPRISE ESTATE
EASTGATE BUSINESS PARK
QUEENSWAY

Superstores
LAKESIDE
RETAIL PARK
P
P Supermarket

Retail Park

Brat Hill

Emmanuel Bridge

Emmanuel Strip

Depot
Raventhorpe Lodge

Low Wood

Holme Hall Golf Course

Sweeting Thorns

1

2

3

BROUGHTON

Wressle

Wressle House

Cemetery

APPLEBY B1207

BRIGG B1208

GREEN LA

B1208 ROAD

RESSLE ROAD

COMMON ROAD

Moor Beck

Watermill Place

Millfield Plantation

WESTMINSTER RD
WESTWOOD
APPLEBY
THE BLACK THORNS
WOODLAND DRIVE
SOUTH TRINITY
LANE
ERMINE STREET

EMERY CL
RAVEN CL
HELON HOLT
BADGER
GARDENS
MILSON
RUE DE NOAY
NOZAY
CHESTNUT GRO
BEECHWOOD CR
TOWN HILL
PINETREE CL
HILLSIDE
EASTWOLD
ELDER DRIVE
FAIRVIEW
VIEW
TOWN WAY
ST BERNARDS CL
ANDALE
DALMATION WAY
BROOKLANDS
YARBOROUGH
SOUTHFIELDS RD
CRAIG CL
SAND LA
BASSETT CL
BEAGLE
DANE CL
BECK LA
CHAPEL RD
CHAPEL
STREET
MILL LANE
GREEN
CATHERINE GRO
GREYFRIARS ROAD
POPLAR DR
BRUCE CL
BURNSIDE
AVENUE
HIGH STREET
SCAWBY
B1207 ROAD

OLD MILL LA
CHANCEL WK
CHAPTER WK
CLOISTER WK

Sch Liby

HIGH STREET

CHURCH LA
CORONATION GDS
Playing Fields
School

STERNE AV
STANWELLS
GREENHILL
LYCH GATE
Hall
ESTATE
SILLWOOD STREET
WYATT AV
GEORGE
DIXON

Broughton

Broomfield Plantation

Sinney Hills Plantation

4

5

6

E   F   G   H

The Index includes some names for which there is insufficient space on the maps. These names are preceded by an * and are followed by the nearest adjoining thoroughfare.

SCUNTHORPE

Abbey Rd. DN17 11 G1
Abbots Rd. DN17 11 G1
Abercorn St. DN16 7 B6
Abey Gdns. DN15 5 F4
Acacia Av. DN15 4 B4
Acacia Ct. DN16 12 B1
Acer Gro. DN17 11 E2
Agard Av. DN15 8 A2
Airedale Rd. DN16 12 C2
Ajax Ct. DN15 5 E4
Alan Cres. DN15 8 B2
Alba Clo. DN17 11 E2
Albert Marson Ct. DN16 7 D6
Albert Rd. DN16 12 A1
Alberta Cres. DN17 11 F3
Albion Pk. DN16 9 F3
Albourne Av. DN15 8 B2
Alexander Rd. DN16 7 D5
Alexandra Rd. DN16 12 A1
Alfreton Ct (42). DN15 6 B2
Allanby St. DN15 7 B2
Almond Gro. DN16 8 D5
Alveston Rd. DN17 6 D4
Alvingham Rd. DN16 8 C5
Amos Cres. DN16 9 F6
Ancaster Ct. DN17 11 H2
Ancholme Rd. DN16 12 C1
Anchor Rd. DN16 13 G2
Anderson Rd. DN16 9 E5
Angerstein Rd. DN17 11 G2
Annes Cres. DN16 9 E6
Appleby Clo. DN17 11 G2
Appleby Mill Rd. DN16 9 G2
Appleton Way. DN16 12 C1
Argyle Ct. DN15 7 B3
Arkwright Way. DN16 9 G6
Armour Rd. DN16 9 G1
Ash Gro. DN16 8 D5
Ashberry Gro. DN16 8 D6
Ashby High St. DN16 12 A1
Ashby Rd. DN16 7 A5
Ashdown Av. DN15 4 D5
Aspen Gro. DN16 8 D5
Asterby Rd. DN17 11 G2
Aston Sq. DN15 4 D6
Atkinsons Way. DN15 4 D2
Atlas Rd. DN17 8 B5
Auckland Rd. DN16 8 B2
Audern Rd. DN16 12 A3
Austin Ct. DN17 11 H4
Avenswood La. DN15 4 B3
Avenue Cannes. DN15 4 C4
Avenue Clamart. DN15 4 C3
Avenue Fontenay. DN15 4 C4
Avenue Lourdes. DN15 4 C4
Avenue Rouen. DN15 4 C4
Avenue Vivian. DN15 4 C5
Avon Rd. DN16 7 D6
Axholme Rd. DN16 8 A2
Aylesby Rd. DN17 11 G2

Baildon Rd. DN15 4 C5
Bakewell Ct. DN15 6 B2
Baldwin Av. DN16 12 A5
Balliol Dri. DN16 12 A3
Balmoral Ct. DN16 11 H3
Banbury Rd. DN16 9 E3
Bardney Av. DN16 8 C6
Barlings Av. DN16 8 C6
Barnes Cres. DN15 4 D5
Barnetby Rd. DN17 11 G2
Barnstaple Rd. DN17 6 C5
Basic Slag Rd. DN16 9 G2
Baslow Rd. DN15 6 B2
Baysdale Rd. DN16 12 C2
Beaford Ct (26). DN17 6 C5
Beauchamp St. DN16 7 D6
Beauchamp Wk. DN16 7 D6

Beauchief Gdns. DN16 8 C5
Beck La. DN16 12 B4
Bedale Rd. DN16 12 D2
Beech Av. DN16 4 A4
Beeches Av. DN16 12 B3
Beechway. DN16 8 D5
Beesby Rd. DN17 11 F2
Belgrave Sq. DN15 7 C3
Bell La. DN15 8 C2
Bellingham Rd. DN16 9 F6
Belmont St. DN16 12 A1
Belper St (46). DN16 6 B2
Belvedere Dri. DN17 8 A5
Bennett Rd. DN16 9 E5
Berkeley St. DN15 7 A2
Bessemer Way. DN15 5 G4
Betony Clo. DN15 4 B3
Betula Way. DN17 11 E2
Beverley Ct. DN17 6 D5
Bideford Ct (7). DN17 6 D5
Bigby Gro. DN16 11 H3
Billet La. DN15 5 E1
Billet Mill App Rd. DN16 9 H6
Billet Mill Rd. DN16 9 F3
Bilsdale Rd. DN16 12 D2
Birchwood Rd. DN16 12 A3
Birkdale Rd. DN17 11 E4
Blackthorn Clo. DN15 4 B3
Blake Av. DN17 8 A6
Blenheim Ct. DN16 12 A4
Bluebell Clo. DN15 7 D4
Bodmin Clo. DN17 6 D4
Bolingbroke Rd. DN17 11 G3
Bolsover Rd. DN15 6 B2
Bonby Gro. DN17 11 H2
Boston App Rd. DN16 13 E1
Bottesford Av. DN16 12 B2
Bottesford La. DN16 12 B2
Bottesford Rd. DN16 12 A1
Boughton Av. DN15 4 D5
Bramley Cres. DN16 12 A4
Brandon Rd. DN15 8 A2
Brankwell Cres. DN17 11 G4
Bransdale Rd. DN16 12 C2
Brant Rd. DN15 8 B2
Brian Av. DN16 12 C2
Briar Way. DN16 4 B3
Bridges Rd. DN17 8 A6
Bridgewater Rd. DN17 6 D4
Bridport Wk. DN17 6 C4
Brigg Rd. DN16 9 E2
Bristol Rd. DN17 6 C4
Brixham Ct (10). DN17 6 D5
Broadway. DN16 12 A1
Brocklesby Rd. DN17 11 G3
Brookdale Rd. DN17 11 E1
Broom Gro. DN16 8 D5
Browning Clo. DN17 8 A6
Brumby Ho. Dri. DN16 8 C5
Brumby Wood La. DN17 6 G3
Brunel Clo. DN16 12 A3
Buckfast Ct (2). DN17 6 D4
Buckingham Av. DN16 5 E3
Buckingham St Nth. DN15 5 E4
Buckingham St Sth. DN15 5 E4
Bude Ct (20). DN17 6 D5
Burdock Rd. DN16 12 C3
Burghley Rd. DN16 9 E5
Burke St. DN15 7 A1
Burke St Nth. DN15 5 F5
Burn Rd. DN15 4 B6
Burnet Dri. DN16 12 C2
Burnham Rd. DN16 8 A2
Burrington Rd. DN17 11 E2
Bushfield Rd. DN16 8 C4
Buxton Ct. DN15 6 B2
Byfield Rd. DN17 11 E1
Byrd Rd. DN16 9 F6
Byron Clo. DN17 8 A6

Caenby Rd. DN17 11 F2
Caistor Av. DN16 12 A3
Calder Rd.DN16 12 C1
Cambridge Av. DN16 12 A3
Camelia Ave. DN16 12 C1
Camomile Clo. DN16 12 D2
Campbell Av. DN16 12 B3
Canterbury Clo. DN17 6 C5

Carisbrooke Manor La. DN17 10 C2
Carlton St. DN15 7 D3
Castella Dri. DN16 9 E2
Castleton Rd. DN15 6 B2
Cathedral Ct. DN17 11 H1
Cavendish Rd. DN16 12 A3
Cecile Cres. DN15 4 D6
Cedar Av. DN15 4 B4
Cemetery Rd. DN16 7 C6
Centenary Cotts. DN15 8 C3
Central Way. DN16 9 F2
Chaffinch Clo. DN15 4 C4
Chancel Rd. DN16 12 A3
Chapel Ct. DN16 7 C2
Chapel St. DN15 7 B2
Chapman Av. DN17 6 D6
Charles Lovell Way. DN17 6 D4
Charterhouse Dri. DN16 12 B3
Chatterton Cres. DN16 5 F4
Chaucer Av. DN17 6 D6
Cheltenham Clo. DN16 12 C3
Chelwood Rd. DN17 8 B6
Cherry Gro. DN16 8 D6
Cherry Mount. DN16 12 B3
Chesney Dri. DN16 12 A4
Chesterfield Rd.DN15 6 B3
Chestnut Way. DN16 8 D5
Chiltern Cres. DN17 6 D5
Church Ct. DN15 7 C2
Church La, Bottesford. DN16 12 B4
Church La, Scunthorpe. DN15 8 A2
Church Sq. DN15 7 D2
Churchfield Rd. DN16 12 B2
Clare Av.DN17 6 D5
Clare Cres. DN16 12 A3
Clarendon Rd. DN17 8 B5
Clarke St. DN15 7 A3
Claxby St. DN17 11 G2
Clayfield Rd. DN16 5 E3
Clematis Way. DN16 12 C3
Clevedon Rd. DN17 6 D5
Cleveland Clo. DN17 6 D5
Cliff Closes Rd. DN15 6 D2
Cliff Gdns. DN15 7 A4
Cliff St. DN16 7 D5
Clovelly Ct (16). DN17 6 D5
Coke Oven Av. DN16 9 G2
Cole St. DN15 7 C2
Coleridge Av. DN17 6 D5
Colin Rd. DN16 9 E3
Collinson Av. DN15 4 B6
Collum Av. DN16 8 D5
Collum Gdns. DN16 12 A1
Collum La. DN16 12 A1
Coltsfoot Clo. DN15 4 B3
Comforts Av. DN16 7 A4
Commercial Rd. DN16 9 E2
Concast Rd. DN16 13 H1
Conference Ct. DN16 12 A5
Conifer Clo. DN17 11 E2
Coningsby Rd. DN17 11 F2
Conway Sq. DN15 4 D6
Copper Beech Wk. DN16 12 B3
Copplestone Ct (27). DN17 6 C5
Copse Rd. DN16 12 A2
Corby Rd. DN16 9 E3
Cornwall Rd. DN16 12 C2
Corporation Rd. DN15 7 B4
Cottage Beck Rd. DN16 7 A6
Coventry Clo. DN17 6 C6
Covert Rd. DN16 12 A1
Cowper Av. DN17 8 A6
Cresta Dri. DN17 11 G3
Crispin Way. DN16 12 A1
Croft La. DN17 11 G5
Cromwell Av. DN16 7 D6
Crosby Av. DN15 5 E3
Crosby Ho. DN15 7 C1
Crosby Rd. DN15 7 B1
Cross St. DN15 7 D2
Crossbeck Rd. DN16 12 A2
Crowberry Rd. DN16 12 C2
Crowland Av. DN16 8 C5
Crowston Wk. DN17 7 C3

Cupola Way. DN15 5 E1
Cuxwold Rd. DN16 9 E5
Dale St. DN15 5 E5
Dale St Nth. DN15 5 E4
Danum Rd. DN17 8 B4
Dartmouth Rd. DN17 6 C4
Davy Av. DN15 4 D5
Dawes La. DN15 9 E1
Dawlish St (36). DN17 6 C5
Deacon Dri. DN15 6 B2
Dean Rd. DN17 11 G1
Denby Clo. DN15 6 B2
Derby Rd. DN15 6 B2
Derwent Rd. DN16 12 C1
Detuyll St. DN15 5 E4
Detuyll St W. DN15 5 E4
Devonshire Rd. DN17 8 B5
Dewsbury Av. DN15 4 B6
Deyne Av. DN15 7 A3
Diana St. DN15 5 F4
Digby St. DN15 5 E5
Dolman Cres. DN17 11 H3
Doncaster Rd. DN15 7 A3
Donnington Gdns. DN15 5 E6
Dorchester Rd. DN17 6 C5
Dovedale Rd. DN16 12 D1
Downing Cres. DN16 12 A3
Dowse Av. DN15 4 D6
Dragonet Rd. DN17 11 G3
Dronfield Ct (39). DN15 6 B2
Dryden Rd. DN17 6 D5
Dudley Rd. DN16 9 F6
Dunlop Way. DN16 9 G6
Dunstall St. DN15 7 A3
Durston Ct (28). DN17 6 C5
Earl St. DN16 7 C6
Earls Wk. DN16 7 C6
East Boundary Rd. DN16 9 H3
East Common La. DN16 8 D4
East Walk. DN15 7 C3
Eastfield Rd. DN16 12 C2
Eastside Rd. DN16 9 G3
Eastwood Ct (44). DN15 6 B2
Eden Dene. DN16 12 D1
Edgemere. DN15 6 B2
Edwards Rd. DN15 5 E5
Elizabeth St. DN15 7 C6
Ellison Av. DN16 11 H5
Elm Gro. DN16 8 D5
Emmanuel Ct. DN16 12 B1
Emmanuel Dri. DN16 12 A4
Emmanuel Rd. DN16 13 E1
Endcliff Av. DN17 11 G5
Enderby Rd. DN17 11 E2
Eryholme Cres. DN15 8 B2
Ethel Ct. DN15 7 C3
*Eton Ct, Park Av. DN17 11 H3
Eton Dri. DN17 11 G4
Everest Rd. DN16 12 B1
Exeter Rd. DN15 8 B2
Exmoor Av. DN15 4 C2
Exmoor Rd. DN17 6 C5
Eyre Av. DN16 12 A1
Fairfield Rd. DN16 4 C5
Fairmont Cres. DN16 7 D6
Falmouth Ct (34). DN17 6 C5
Fardell Rd. DN16 9 E5
Farthing Av. DN15 4 D6
Fenton St. DN15 7 C3
Ferriby Rd. DN17 11 F2
Fern Lea Clo. DN 8 B3
Ferry Rd. DN15 4 C4
Ferry Rd West. DN15 4 A3
Fifth Av. DN17 6 B6
Fillingham Rd. DN15 4 A6
Fir Clo. DN16 11 H3
First Av, Ashfield Caravan Pk. DN17 10 D1
First Av, Parklands Caravan Site. DN17 6 C6
Fletcher Clo.DN15 4 B3
Flixborough Ftpth. DN15 7 C3
Fotherby Rd. DN15 11 G3
Fourth Av. DN17 6 B6

Fowler Rd. DN16 8 D5
Fox St. DN15 7 A2
Foxhills Rd. DN15 4 D4
Frances St. DN15 7 B2
Franklin Cres. DN16 9 F6
Friars Rd. DN17 11 G1
Frodingham Ftpth. DN15 7 C3
Frodingham Rd. DN15 7 A1
Frodingham Sth Rd. DN16 9 G4
Fulbeck Rd. DN16 9 E6
Fuchsia Croft. DN15 8 B3
George St. DN15 7 B1
Gervase St. DN15 8 B1
Giblin Cotts. DN15 4 D5
Gilliatt St. DN15 7 B2
Girton Clo. DN16 12 A3
Gladstone Dri. DN16 9 E3
Glaisdale Rd. DN16 12 D2
Glanford Rd. DN17 11 G4
Glanford Way. DN16 4 A6
Glanville Av. DN17 8 B4
Glanville Cres. DN17 8 B5
Glebe Rd. DN15 7 B1
Glossop Rd. DN16 6 B2
Gloucester Av. DN16 8 D5
Glover Rd. DN17 8 B4
Goldcrest Clo. DN15 4 C3
Goodwood. DN17 11 F3
Gorse Clo. DN16 12 C3
Grammar School Wk. DN16 12 B3
Grange Av. DN16 5 F4
Grange La Nth. DN16 9 F6
Grange La Sth. DN16 12 C1
Grasby Rd. DN17 11 F2
Grassmoor Ct (43). DN15 6 B2
Gray Rd. DN17 6 D6
Greengarth. DN17 11 G5
Greenhide Rd. DN17 11 E3
Greens Clo. DN15 7 D3
Grosvenor St Nth. DN15 7 B1
Grosvenor St Sth. DN15 7 B1
Gunby Rd. DN17 11 F2
Gurnell St. DN15 7 B2
Haig Av. DN16 7 C6
Hales Clo. DN16 11 H5
Hallbrook Ct. DN16 11 H6
Hallgarth Av. DN17 7 C5
Hamilton Rd. DN17 8 B4
Hammerton Rd. DN17 11 G3
Hampton Rd. DN16 8 D4
Hanover Gdns. DN16 12 C1
Hardy Rd. DN17 6 D6
Hargreaves Way. DN15 5 G3
Harrow Gdns. DN17 11 G5
Hartland Ct (13). DN17 6 D5
Hartshead Av. DN15 4 B6
Hathersage Ct (45). DN15 6 B2
Haworth Clo. DN15 4 C5
Hawthorne Av. DN17 8 B5
Hawthorne Cres. DN17 8 B5
Hayle Ct (9). DN17 6 D5
Headley Rd. DN16 9 E5
Heanor Ct. DN15 6 B2
Heather Gro. DN16 12 D2
Hebden Rd. DN15 4 B5
Helston Wk. DN17 6 C4
Hempdyke Rd. DN15 4 D5
Henderson Av. DN15 5 E5
Henderson Cres. DN15 5 E5
Henry St. DN15 8 B1
Hereward Pl. DN16 9 F6
Heron Clo. DN15 4 B3
Herrick Rd. DN16 9 F6
Herriot Way. DN16 6 C1
Hibston Clo. DN16 12 A5
High Garth. DN17 11 G5
High Leys Rd. DN17 11 G3
High St, Scunthorpe. DN15 7 A3
High St, Yaddlethorpe. DN17 11 G4
High St East. DN15 7 D2
Highcliff Gdns. DN15 4 D6
Highfield Av. DN15 8 A2

Hillary Rd. DN16 12 B2
Hillfoot Dri. DN17 11 G4
Hilltop Av. DN15 4 C4
Hilton Av. DN15 4 A6
Hindon Wk. DN17 6 C4
Hinman Wk. DN15 7 C3
Holgate Rd. DN16 9 E5
Holland Av. DN15 4 D5
Holly Clo. DN16 12 C3
Holme Hall Av. DN16 12 B4
Holme La. DN16 12 B4
Holmfirth Rd. DN16 4 B5
Holstein Dri. DN16 11 H5
Holyrood Dri. DN15 4 C2
Home St. DN15 7 C1
Honeysuckle Ct. DN16 12 C3
Hood Rd. DN17 6 D6
Hopkins Av. DN17 8 C5
Horbury Clo. DN15 4 C5
Hornbeam Av. DN16 11 H2
Hornsby Cres. DN15 5 E4
Hoylake Rd. DN17 11 E4
Hudson Av. DN15 4 D4
Humber Cres. DN17 8 B6
Hunt Rd. DN16 12 B2
Hurst La. DN17 11 G4

Ilkeston Ct (38). DN15 6 B2
INDUSTRIAL & RETAIL:
 Berkeley Ind Est. DN15 4 B4
 Eastgate Business Pk.
  DN16 13 E1
 Foxhills Ind Est. DN15 5 E2
 Grange Ind Est. DN16 9 F5
 Kingsway Hi-Tech
  Business Pk. DN17 8 A4
 Lakeside Retail Pk.
  DN16 13 E1
 Lysaghts Enterprise Pk.
  DN15 5 E1
 Midland Ind Est. DN16 9 E3
 Moorwell Business Pk.
  DN17 11 F4
 New Brumby Ind Est.
  DN16 9 F5
 Queensway Enterprise Est.
  DN16 13 E1
 Sawcliffe Ind Pk.
  DN15 5 G3
 Skippingdale Ind Pk.
  DN15 4 C2
 South Park Ind Est.
  DN17 11 E4
Inglewood Ct. DN16 11 H3
Irby Rd. DN17 11 G2
Irvine Rd. DN16 12 C2
Ivanhoe Rd. DN16 9 E4

Jacklins App. DN16 12 A4
Jackson Rd. DN16 4 D6
Jellicoe Ct. DN16 9 E4
John St. DN15 7 C3
Jonquil Av. DN16 12 C2
Jubilee Cotts. DN15 8 C3
Juniper Clo. DN15 4 B3

Kathleen Av. DN16 12 B2
Keats Av. DN17 6 D6
Keddington Rd. DN17 11 H3
Keelby Rd. DN17 11 G2
Kelsey Av. DN15 4 A6
Kendale Rd. DN17 9 F2
Kendall Ct. DN16 12 B1
Kenilworth Rd. DN16 4 A6
Kensington Rd. DN15 11 G5
Kenya Dri. DN17 11 H5
Kestrel Rd. DN17 11 F1
Kettering Rd. DN16 9 E3
Keynsham Ct (19). DN17 6 C5
King Edward St. DN16 7 B6
King St. DN15 7 C1
Kingerby Rd. DN17 11 G2
Kingfisher Clo. DN15 4 C4
Kings Ct. DN15 7 C1
Kingsdale. DN17 11 G5
Kingston Rd. DN16 8 C5
Kingsway. DN17 6 C2
Kingsway Service Rd.
 DN15 4 C6
Kinsley Wk. DN15 7 C3
Kipling Av. DN16 8 B5
Kirkby Rd. DN17 11 G3
Kirnan Cres. DN17 11 G4
Knights Ct. DN16 12 A4

Laburnum Gro. DN16 8 D6

Lacey Rd. DN17 11 G2
Lagoon Rd. DN17 6 B6
Lakeside Dri. DN17 11 E2
Lakeside Parkway.
 DN16 13 E1
Lambourne Rise. DN16 12 A5
Lammerton Ct (14).
 DN17 6 D5
Lancaster Rd. DN16 12 A2
Landoor Av. DN17 6 D5
Laneham St. DN15 7 B3
Langley Dri. DN16 11 H5
Larch Gro. DN16 8 D5
Lavender Way. DN15 7 D4
Lawnswood Ct. DN16 12 A3
Laxton Gro. DN16 11 H5
Leamington Clo. DN16 9 E4
Leamington Ct. DN16 9 E4
Lee Fair Gdns. DN17 11 H4
Legard Av. DN16 12 A1
Leonard Cres. DN16 8 B2
Leopold Clo. DN16 12 A1
Leslie Clo. DN16 7 C3
Leven Rd. DN16 12 D1
Lichfield Av. DN17 6 C6
Lilac Av. DN16 9 E4
Lime Av. DN16 13 E1
Lime Gro. DN16 8 D5
Lincoln Ct. DN16 8 D5
Lincoln Gdns. DN16 8 C6
Lindley St. DN16 12 A1
Lindsey St. DN16 7 D5
Lindum St. DN15 7 C3
Linnet Clo. DN16 4 C3
Liscombe Ct (21). DN17 6 D5
Lister Rd. DN16 4 B6
Little John St. DN15 7 C3
Lloyds Av. DN17 8 B4
Lockwood Ct. DN15 4 D5
Lodge Rd. DN15 6 B2
Long Rd. DN16 4 D5
Lovell Rd. DN17 11 F3
Low Garth. DN17 11 G5
Low Leys Rd. DN17 11 F3
Lulworth Ct (37). DN17 6 C5
Luneburg Pl. DN15 4 B4
Luneburg Way. DN15 4 B3
Lunedale Rd. DN16 12 D2
Lydbrook Rd. DN16 8 C3
Lydford Ct (4). DN17 6 D4
Lygon St. DN16 7 C6
Lyndale Gdns. DN16 8 D6
Lynmouth Dri. DN17 6 C4
Lynton Clo. DN15 4 C5
Lysaghts Way. DN15 5 E1

Mackender Ct. DN16 12 B1
Magdalen Clo. DN16 12 A3
Magnolia Way. DN16 8 C5
Main App Rd. DN16 9 E2
Main Rd. DN17 10 D1
Maine Av. DN16 4 B4
Mallalieu Ct. DN15 4 D5
Mallard Rd. DN17 11 F1
Malling Wk. DN16 12 A5
Mallory Rd. DN16 12 C2
Maltby Rd. DN17 11 F2
Malvern Rd. DN17 8 B5
Manby Rd. DN17 11 F3
Manifold Rd. DN16 12 C2
Manley St. DN15 7 D3
Mannaberg Way. DN15 5 F3
Manor Farm Rd. DN17 11 F1
Manor Rd. DN16 12 A4
Mansfield Rd. DN15 6 B2
Maple Av. DN15 4 B4
Maple Tree Clo E. DN16 8 C4
Maple Tree Clo W. DN16 8 C4
Maple Tree Way. DN16 7 B6
Market Hill. DN16 7 C2
Marlborough Dri. DN16 12 A4
Marlowe Rd. DN17 6 C6
Marmion Rd. DN16 8 D5
Marsden Dri. DN16 4 C6
Marshfield Rd. DN16 12 C2
Mary St. DN15 7 A3
Mary Sumner Way.
 DN15 4 D5
Mason Dri. DN17 11 F4
Matlock Ct. DN15 6 B2
Mavis Rd. DN15 11 F1
Meadow Rd. DN17 11 E1
Melbury Wk. DN17 6 C4
Melford Rd. DN16 12 D2
Menasha Way. DN16 9 G6
Mendip Rd. DN17 6 D4

Mercia Way. DN15 5 E2
Mere Cres. DN16 9 E6
Meredith Av. DN16 7 C6
Merlin Rd. DN17 11 F1
Merries Wk. DN17 6 C4
Merryweather Ct. DN16 12 A5
Merton Rd. DN16 12 A3
Messingham Rd. DN17 11 H1
Middleton Rd. DN16 12 A3
Midland Rd. DN16 9 E3
Mill Croft. DN16 9 F5
Mill Field Rd. DN16 9 F2
Mill Hill Dri. DN16 12 B4
Milton Rd. DN16 12 B2
Minster Rd. DN15 6 B2
Mirfield Rd. DN16 4 B5
Modder St. DN16 12 A1
Monks Rd. DN17 11 H1
Montrose St. DN16 7 B6
Moor Rd. DN17 10 D5
Moors Rd. DN16 6 B2
Moorwell Rd. DN17 11 E5
Morecambe Av. DN16 12 A2
Morley Rd. DN17 11 G2
Mountbatten Clo. DN16 12 A3
Mulgrave St. DN15 7 A1

Neath Rd. DN16 8 C3
Neville Rd. DN16 7 D5
New Rd. DN17 10 D1
Newbolt Av. DN17 6 D5
Newborn Av. DN16 4 D5
Newbury Ct (6). DN17 6 C5
Newcomen Way. DN15 5 G3
Newdown Rd. DN17 11 F4
Newland Av. DN15 8 A2
Newland Dri. DN15 8 A2
Newland Wk. DN15 8 A2
Newnham Cres. DN16 11 H3
Newton Rd. DN16 12 D1
Nightingale Clo. DN15 4 C4
Nine Chimneys Rd.
 DN16 9 F2
Norman Clo. DN17 8 B5
Normanby Rd. DN15 7 B3
North Farm Rd. DN17 11 F4
North Lincoln Rd. DN16 9 F3
North Par. DN16 12 C1
North St. DN15 7 D1
Northampton Rd. DN16 9 E4
Northfield Clo. DN16 8 D6
Northolme Cres. DN15 8 A2
Norton Rd. DN16 12 B2
Norwood Av. DN15 4 D5
Nostell Rd. DN16 9 F3
Nuffield Clo. DN16 12 A3
Nuns Rd. DN17 11 H1
Nursery Clo. DN17 11 H4

Oak Rd. DN16 8 D5
Oakford Clo. DN17 6 D4
Oakleigh. DN16 12 C4
Oakwood Rd. DN16 12 A2
Ogilvy Dri. DN17 11 G4
Okehampton Ct (25).
 DN17 6 C5
Old Brumby St. DN16 8 C5
Old Crosby. DN15 5 F4
Old Ironside Rd. DN16 9 E2
Old Rectory Gdns.
 DN17 11 H4
Old School La. DN16 12 B4
Ontario Rd. DN17 11 F4
Orb La. DN15 5 F2
Orchard Clo. DN16 12 B4
Orchid Rise. DN15 8 B2
Oriole Rd. DN17 11 F1
Ormsby Rd. DN17 11 F2
Oswald Rd. DN15 7 A3
Ottawa Rd. DN17 11 F3
Oundle Clo. DN16 12 B3
Oxford St. DN16 12 C1

Padstow Wk (22). DN17 6 D5
Park Av. DN17 11 G3
Park Ct. DN15 7 C2
Park Farm Rd. DN15 5 E1
Parkers La. DN16 9 F1
Parkin Rd. DN17 11 H3
Parkinson St. DN15 7 A2
Partridge Clo. DN17 11 G1
Pavilion Gdns. DN15 8 C3
Peacock St. DN17 11 F4
Pembroke Av. DN16 12 A4
Penrose Ct (8). DN17 6 D5
Percival St. DN15 7 A2

Percy St. DN16 7 D5
Peterborough Rd. DN16 8 D5
Peveril Av. DN17 8 B4
Pheasant Clo. DN17 11 G1
Philips Cres. DN15 8 B2
Phoenix Parkway. DN15 4 C3
Pimpernel Way. DN16 12 C2
Pinchbeck Av. DN16 9 E2
Pippin Ct. DN15 4 B4
Pippin Dri. DN16 12 A5
Plantain Clo. DN16 12 C3
Plum Tree Way. DN16 7 B6
Plymouth Rd. DN17 6 C4
Poole Dri. DN17 11 G3
Poppy Clo. DN15 4 B3
Porlock Ct (35). DN17 6 C5
Porter St. DN15 7 A2
Portman Rd. DN15 4 D3
Powells Cres. DN16 12 B1
Primrose Way. DN16 8 B3
Princess Alexandra Ct.
 DN17 11 H3
Prioress Ho. DN15 7 C1
Priory Cres. DN17 8 C6
Priory La. DN17 8 B6
Priory Rd. DN17 11 H1
Pryme Rd. DN16 9 E5
Purbeck Rd. DN17 6 C4

Quantock Clo. DN17 6 D4
Quebec Rd. DN17 11 F3
Queen St. DN16 9 E2
Queens App. DN16 9 G3
Queens Vw Cres. DN16 9 F5
Queensway. DN16 8 C4
Queenswood Rd. DN16 12 B4

Radstock Ct (11). DN17 6 D5
Ram Blvd. DN15 4 D2
Ranby Rd. DN17 11 G2
Ravendale St. DN15 7 B3
Raymond Rd. DN16 9 E6
Redbourn Clo. DN16 8 D4
Redbourn St. DN16 7 D5
Redbourn Way. DN16 7 C6
Redwood Ct. DN16 12 D4
Refinery Rd. DN16 9 G2
Reginald Rd. DN15 4 D4
Repton Dri. DN16 12 B4
Revesby Av. DN16 8 C5
Revesby Ct. DN16 8 C5
Riby Rd. DN17 11 F2
Richmond Dri. DN16 12 A5
Rileston Pl. DN16 12 A5
Riley Ct. DN15 6 B2
Ringwood Clo. DN16 12 A2
Ripon Clo. DN17 6 C6
Rivelin Cres. DN16 8 C5
Rivelin Pl. DN16 8 C5
Rivelin Rd. DN16 8 C5
Riverdale Rd. DN16 8 C5
Robert St. DN15 7 B3
Robinson Clo. DN15 4 D5
Rochdale Rd. DN16 12 A2
Rochester Clo. DN17 6 C5
Rod Mill Rd. DN16 9 G3
Rose Walk. DN15 7 D4
Rosedale. DN17 11 G5
Rosemount Dri. DN16 8 D6
Rosewood Way. DN16 12 B3
Rossall Clo. DN16 12 B4
Rothbury Rd. DN17 8 B6
Rothwell Rd. DN15 4 C5
Rowan Cres. DN16 12 B4
Rowills Rd. DN16 9 E5
Rowlands Rd. DN16 7 A6
Rugby Rd. DN16 8 C4
Russet Clo. DN15 4 B4
Rutland Rd. DN16 9 E5

St Albans Clo. DN17 6 C6
St Andrews Av. DN17 11 H4
St Augustine Cres.
 DN16 12 A2
St Botolphs Rd. DN15 9 E5
St Catherines Cres.
 DN17 6 D4
St Chads Rd. DN16 9 F6
St Davids Cres. DN17 11 F4
St Hughs Cres. DN16 9 E5
St James Ct. DN15 7 A4
St Johns Rd. DN16 12 C1
St Lawrences Pl. DN16 9 F6
St Lawrences Rd. DN16 9 F6
St Margarets Wk. DN16 12 B2

St Marys Ct. DN15 4 B3
St Michaels Cres. DN16 9 E5
St Pauls Rd. DN16 12 B1
St Peters Av. DN16 12 A4
St Vincents Av. DN15 5 F3
Salcombe Ct (12). DN17 6 C5
Salisbury Clo. DN17 6 C5
Salmonby Rd. DN17 11 F2
Sandfield Clo. DN17 11 E2
Sandhouse Cres. DN16 9 E4
Sandringham Cres.
 DN17 11 G4
Saxby Rd. DN17 11 F2
Saxon Ct. DN16 12 A4
Scawby Rd. DN17 11 G2
School Rd. DN16 12 B1
Scot Av. DN17 6 C6
Scotter Rd Sth. DN17 11 E2
Scotter Rd. DN15 4 B6
Scrap Bay Rd. DN16 13 G2
Seabrook Dri. DN16 11 H5
Searby Rd. DN17 11 F3
Seaton Rd. DN17 6 D5
Second Av. DN17 6 C6
Sedgewood Way. DN15 4 B3
Selby Ct. DN17 6 D5
Seraphim App Rd. DN16 9 F3
Seraphim Rd. DN16 9 G4
Services Rd. DN16 9 F2
Shaftesbury Ct (18).
 DN17 6 C5
Shakespeare Av. DN17 6 C6
Sheffield Park Av. DN15 5 E4
Sheffield St. DN15 7 A1
Sheffield St E. DN15 7 A1
Sheffield St W. DN15 7 A1
Shelford St. DN15 7 B3
Shelroy Clo. DN16 5 B4
Sherburn Cres. DN15 4 C5
Sherwood Vale. DN15 4 C6
Shipton Rd. DN16 12 B2
Shirley Cres. DN16 8 D5
Sidney Rd. DN17 6 C6
Silica Cres. DN17 11 E2
Silver Birch Rise. DN16 12 B4
Siskin Cres. DN16 12 B5
Sixth Av. DN16 6 B6
Skelton Rd. DN17 6 C6
Skippingdale Rd. DN15 5 E3
Skylark Rise. DN16 12 B5
Smith St. DN15 7 A2
Smithfield Rd. DN16 12 C1
Snowdonia Av. DN16 4 C2
Somerby Rd. DN17 11 F2
Somervell Rd. DN16 12 C2
Sorrel Way. DN15 4 B3
Southgate. DN15 7 C2
South Pk Rd. DN17 11 E4
South Ridge Cres.
 DN17 11 G4
Southfield Rd. DN16 8 D6
Spalding Rd. DN16 8 C5
Speedwell Cres. DN15 4 B3
Spencer Av. DN15 5 E4
Spilsby Av. DN17 11 F2
Springfield Clo. DN16 8 D6
Staindale Rd. DN16 12 D2
Stainton Dri. DN17 11 F3
Stanley Rd. DN15 4 B6
Station Rd. DN15 7 A5
Stockshill Rd. DN16 9 E6
Stow Rd. DN16 8 C6
Stratford Dri. DN16 7 D6
Stratton Ct (5). DN17 6 D4
Stuart Clo. DN17 11 H4
Sturmer Ct. DN16 12 A4
Sunningdale Rd. DN17 11 F3
Sunway Gro. DN16 12 A2
Sutton Rd. DN15 7 C1
Swaledale Pl. DN16 12 D1
Swift Rd. DN16 7 C6
Swinburne Rd. DN16 6 D6
Swindon Ct (15). DN17 6 D5

Talbot Av. DN16 7 D6
Talisman Av. DN15 4 A6
Tamar Wk. DN17 6 C4
Tamarisk Way. DN16 12 D2
Tanashi Dori. DN17 8 A4
Tavener Ct (40). DN15 6 B2
Tavistock Ct (24). DN17 6 C5
Tealby Rd. DN17 11 F2
Teale St. DN15 7 A2
Teignmouth Ct (1). DN17 6 D4
Temper Rd. DN16 9 H4

15